A DEVOT...

DARKNESS THEN LIGHT

STORIES OF ILLUMINATION
FOR THE SEASON OF ADVENT

CHRISTIANITY TODAY

DARKNESS THEN LIGHT:
Stories of Illumination for the Season of Advent

Copyright © 2025 Christianity Today. All rights reserved.

Christianity Today, P.O. Box 788, Wheaton, IL 60187
ChristianityToday.com
Printed in the USA

EDITOR
Ronnie Martin

EXECUTIVE DIRECTOR
Joy Allmond

CREATIVE DIRECTOR
Alecia Sharp

COPY EDITOR
Tracey Moore

ILLUSTRATOR
Jill DeHaan

Unless otherwise indicated, Scripture taken from the Holy Bible, NEW INTERNATIONAL VERSION®, NIV® Copyright © 1973, 1978, 1984, 2011 by Biblica, Inc.® Used by permission. All rights reserved worldwide.

Scripture quotations marked (CSB) are taken from the Christian Standard Bible®, copyright © 2017 by Holman Bible Publishers. Used by permission. Christian Standard Bible® and CSB® are federally registered trademarks of Holman Bible Publishers.

Scripture quotations marked (ESV) are from the ESV® Bible (The Holy Bible, English Standard Version®), copyright © 2001 by Crossway, a publishing ministry of Good News Publishers. Used by permission. All rights reserved.

CONTENTS

4
INTRODUCTION

8
WEEK 1
LIGHT DAWNS IN THE DARKNESS

40
WEEK 2
ON THEM HAS LIGHT SHONE

72
WEEK 3
EVEN THE DARKNESS IS NOT DARK

104
WEEK 4
THE LIGHT OF LIFE

… INTRODUCTION

DARKNESS THEN LIGHT

RONNIE MARTIN

Christmastime has arrived in all its luster, but I'm having one of those nights when sleeping has become a wild ambition. The cares of the world are weighing down on my soul, and the ticking hand of my analog clock has turned into a deafening roar. For me, it is better to simply admit defeat and abandon any hope of attaining some sweet slumber. I silently shuffle down the dim hallway, trying to keep my steps delicate as the Christmas tree finally comes into view from the corner of the room. I glance at the garland and lights, woven between the pine needles in suspended animation, still magically twinkling from the night before. Even in this depressingly early hour, it manages to bring a faint smile to my sleepy face.

Of course, this is predawn, when everything appears darker and quieter than at any other time of the day. I settle into a room we call the library and gaze through the glass windowpane as the first hints of light declare morning's arrival. Although my eyes are tired and dull, my mind happens to be as alert as ever. As I sit before the Lord in stillness, he provides me with a much-needed remembrance at Christmastime: My story is not always what it seems. It appears darker and quieter at times. It feels lost in a forest of shadows and obscured images. What I'm learning is that these are the predawn moments of my life.

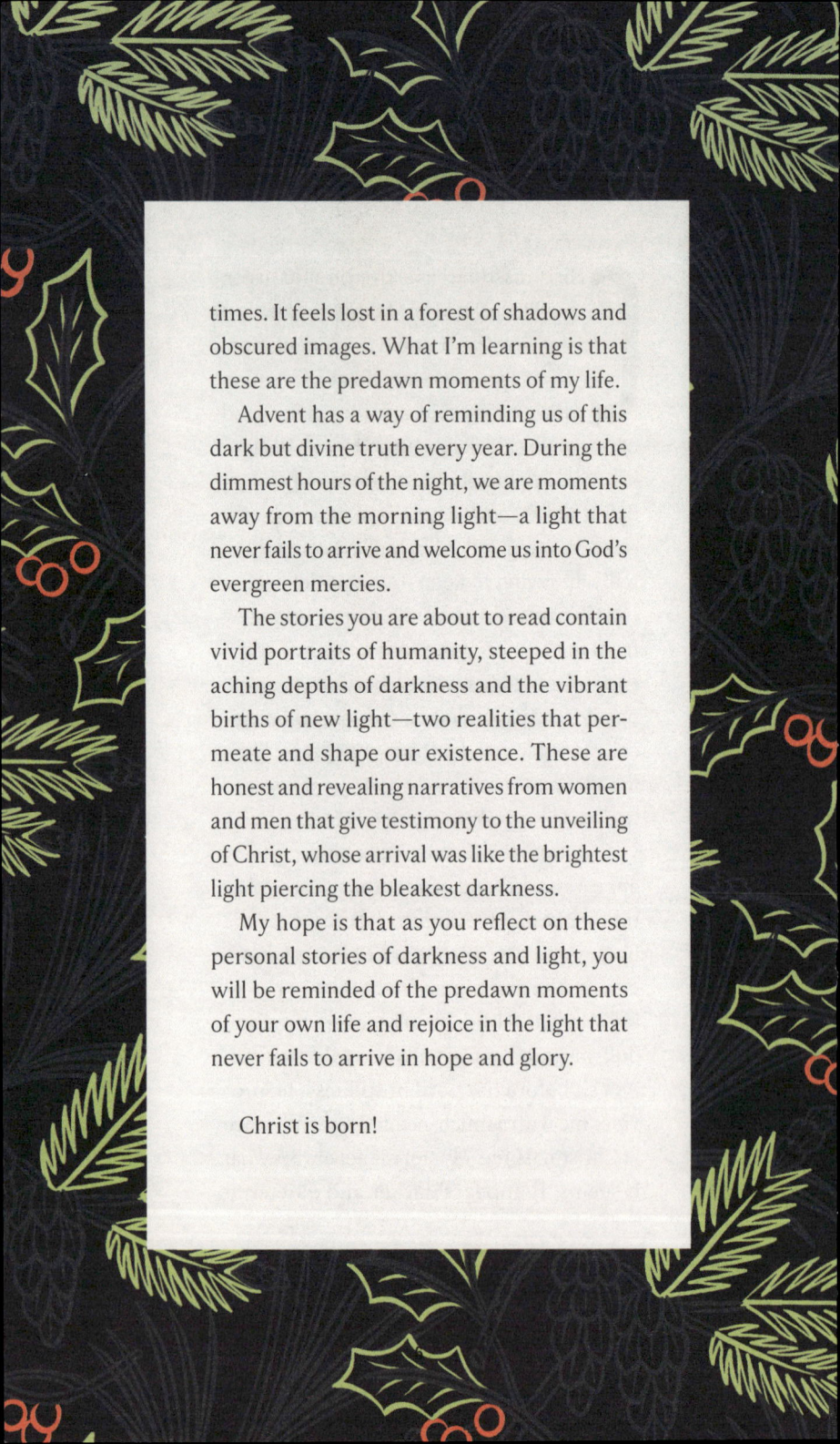

Advent has a way of reminding us of this dark but divine truth every year. During the dimmest hours of the night, we are moments away from the morning light—a light that never fails to arrive and welcome us into God's evergreen mercies.

The stories you are about to read contain vivid portraits of humanity, steeped in the aching depths of darkness and the vibrant births of new light—two realities that permeate and shape our existence. These are honest and revealing narratives from women and men that give testimony to the unveiling of Christ, whose arrival was like the brightest light piercing the bleakest darkness.

My hope is that as you reflect on these personal stories of darkness and light, you will be reminded of the predawn moments of your own life and rejoice in the light that never fails to arrive in hope and glory.

Christ is born!

WEEK 1

The Son of God became a man to enable men to become sons of God.
C.S. LEWIS

Light dawns in the darkness for the upright; he *is* gracious, merciful, and righteous.

PSALM 112:4

ESV

WI|DI

LET THERE BE HOPE

CHAD BIRD

is a scholar in residence at 1517. He is the cohost of the podcast *40 Minutes in the Old Testament* and the author of several books, including *Untamed Prayers: 365 Daily Devotions on Christ in the Book of Psalms*.

Midnight stole upon us while the sun remained high in the sky. It was a Saturday. The phone rang. I answered. And just like that, night fell. Words upon words, like soot-black spatters of darkness, rained from the phone and smothered me.

It was the call that other parents get. You know, the ones of whom we say, "Oh, those poor parents. My heart breaks for them." Only it was not other parents. Not this time. And the heart crushed and ground to fragmentary shards lay dead but stubbornly alive within my own chest.

Luke had fallen to his death. A sentence grammatically simple. A fact devastatingly horrid. On this side of the resurrection, he will remain, with every passing year, 21 years old.

He had died on a hike while studying abroad in Chile. In the weeks we waited for his body to be flown home, in the time between his funeral at home and his second funeral and interment at the United States Naval Academy, and in the months following, I arose early and walked for miles in the dark. Praying psalms. Weeping rivers of tears. Launching a million and one whys to heaven's throne of grace.

Day by torturous day, unbeknown to me at first, the Spirit of God was doing what he has been doing since the dawn of life: accomplishing his best work in the dark. The Lord's creation of all things began in the dark. "Let there be light," he said, and there was light. His creation of each of us began in the darkness of the womb. "Let there be birth," he said, and there was birth.

Within me, the voice that spoke, initially in a whisper but with gradually intensifying volume, uttered these four words: "Let there be hope." And there was hope.

Our Father was accomplishing his work within me in the dark. He taught me, when the present is covered with the shadow of death, to borrow light from the past. There is hope because the young man whose body we buried had been united by baptism to the living body of Jesus, who had also been buried, then rose triumphant, his foot on the neck of death for us.

The Lord taught me to bank on light from the future as well, for no matter how fierce the growl of midnight grief, it whimpers in defeat when dawn begins to laugh. And the dawn of resurrection comes. It shone during the first advent of Jesus, when he vacated his borrowed tomb, and that resurrection dawn will dispel every vestige of night at his second coming.

I have learned that tears and smiles can coexist in a soul full of the hope of what Jesus has done, is doing, and will do for us. Never will I be the same, and I am grateful for that. Through wounds and tears, in darkness and grief, I have learned that "even the darkness will not be dark to you," O Christ (Ps. 139:12), for you are the Light of the World.

NO MATTER HOW FIERCE
THE GROWL OF MIDNIGHT GRIEF,
IT WHIMPERS IN DEFEAT WHEN
DAWN BEGINS TO LAUGH.

W1 | D2

CHRISTMAS IN WARTIME

DANIEL DARLING

is an author and pastor. He is the director of the Land Center for Cultural Engagement at Southwestern Seminary and author of several books, including *The Characters of Christmas*.

We drove down busy streets, sirens intermittently breaking up the feigned normalcy of a city in wartime. Ukrainians worked and shopped, worshiped and worried throughout Kyiv, miles from the front but seconds from a missile strike.

We toured a children's hospital with an entire ward reduced to a pile of rubble, the target of a Russian bomber. We visited an underground shelter where students, at a moment's notice, could leave their desks and go study while the world burned. We spoke with Ukrainian children rescued from kidnapping and exploitation by the Russians and now cared for by an evangelical Christian ministry.

But it was the final scene in Kyiv last December that brought a steady flow of tears to my eyes. As we dragged our luggage through the train station and readied ourselves to board for an overnight trip to Krakow, we heard a Ukrainian band belting out Christmas carols. It seemed an act of defiance by these sturdy people, as if to say, *We will celebrate Christmas. Not even war will erase our hope.*

The festivity and joy of this season is always, every year, juxtaposed with the backdrop of brokenness. This year is no different. Economic uncertainty in the West. Civil war, again, in Sudan. A Middle East aflame.

How can Christians possibly, audaciously, pause for Advent in a world so dark? A lyric of a favorite hymn says it clearly: "A thrill of hope, the weary world rejoices." The birth of Jesus came at a time no less troubled than our own, to a people pressed down and weary, to a world on edge. Accompanying Jesus' birth was the jealous slaughter of young boys by the mad monarch, Herod. Violence. Poverty. Corruption.

When will this cycle ever end? Yet those who believed knew the birth of this baby boy to a peasant couple was the beginning of something new. Zechariah said as much in his prayer:

> Because of our God's merciful compassion,
> the dawn from on high will visit us
> to shine on those who live in darkness
> and the shadow of death,
> to guide our feet into the way of peace.
> (Luke 1:78–79, CSB)

As the prophet Isaiah foretold, those who have walked in darkness will now see a great light. This Light, John would later write, has come into the world and the darkness will not overcome it. It will not overcome him.

You may not be feeling the light this Christmas. Your world may seem dreary, full of grief and woe. I've known this feeling. I've walked among those who could see only darkness. Yet Advent offers us genuine hope inside our groaning. God became flesh, inhabited our world, and—by his life, death, and resurrection—defeated the darkness that envelops the world, envelops us.

It's audacious, really, to celebrate Christmas, to sing "Joy to the World" in the midst of war. We can, though, for we know that the baby who lay in that dark cave is the King of the world. He is light, and in him is no darkness at all. A new world awaits.

W1|D3

THE CHRISTMAS CLOUD

DAVE HARVEY

(DMin, WTS) is the president of Great Commission Collective and serves on the board of Christian Counseling & Educational Foundation (CCEF). His most recent book is *The Clay Pot Conspiracy: God's Plan to Use Weakness in Leaders*, and he writes regularly at Revdaveharvey.com.

Call it the "Christmas cloud"—that unwelcome shadow suspended over many in December. For the Christian, it's hard to admit. Who wants to be the Grinch throwing cloud shade on Christ's birthday? After all, "it's the hap-, happiest season of all," right? But for too many, happiness describes our songs, not our souls.

We feel emotionally exiled to the outdoors—peering through frosted windows at friends and families enjoying Christmas cheer. Inside is warmth and wonder. Outside, we're wrapped in scarves of sadness. We wonder, *God became man to save my soul—so why doesn't that touch my happy place?*

Christmas feels decidedly unmerry when our emotions don't align with truth. No one told us life might include decking the halls while feeling dark, displaced, and shame-laced. We ask, *Why does Christmas make me feel more alienated from the very things I know are good? How do I get out from under the cloud?*

Start here: Christmas clouds don't erase light.

Clouds may block the sun so we don't see or feel its effects. But the sun's power isn't compromised. As a Floridian, I know this. We have two seasons: hurricane season and whatever you call the other six months. But even when storms loom, every Floridian knows the sun is still there. When entombed by ominous clouds, sunshine remains an unstoppable reality.

Same with Christmas. It's not first a feeling; it's a fact. "In him was life, and the life was the light of men. The light shines in the darkness, and the darkness has not overcome it" (John 1:4–5, ESV throughout).

The King of light invaded our darkness. He came as light-embodied and light-dispensing. "The true light, which gives light to everyone, was coming into the world" (v. 9). Christ was simultaneously light and lighter.

Don't reduce Christmas to how you feel. I'm not saying ignore emotions—but don't anchor your celebration to them. What makes Christmas merry isn't your mood. It's that Christ's light is true. And he gave it to you.

Remember, you didn't receive Christ as an ever-present emotion. You didn't become a follower of a feeling. Something far greater happened. "God, who said, 'Let light shine out of darkness,' has shone in our hearts to give the light of the knowledge of the glory of God in the face of Jesus Christ" (2 Cor. 4:6). Beams of gospel light pierced your clouded heart. The cloud parted, if only for a moment. You responded to the gospel. The Light won.

So let Christmas remind you: When light and darkness clash, light wins. Every time. And if this Christmas feels too cloudy, reach back to the clarity of when Christ first came to you.

Also remember: Christmas clouds remind us we're not home yet.

No holiday romances our imagination more than Christmas. But this isn't heaven—not even close. Maybe your cloud points to something more holy: You're homesick.

THE SEASON BECOMES GOD'S ANNUAL REMINDER THAT WE'RE NOT HOME YET.

During Christmas, we're pinged by a distant homeland. The season becomes God's annual reminder that we're not home yet. A new earth is ordered and on the way. Christmas incites longings to be whole with friends and family—to be fully known, forever loved, physically whole, and eternally safe. Christmas stirs an emotional foretaste of what will soon be fully satisfied. Proceed through the season "knowing that he who raised the Lord Jesus will raise us also with Jesus and bring us with you into his presence" (2 Cor. 4:14).

So don't curse the Christmas cloud—let it direct your gaze. Christ has come. Christ is here. Christ will come again.

That's not a feeling. That's a fact bright enough to break through any cloud.

W1|D4

HOLD ON, DEAR PILGRIM, HOLD ON

W. DAVID O. TAYLOR

is associate professor of theology and culture at Fuller Theological Seminary and the author of *Open and Unafraid*, *A Body of Praise*, and *Prayers for the Pilgrimage*. He posts about art and theology @davidtaylor_theologian on Instagram.

I once lived in a neighborhood where the pecan trees rose a hundred feet high into the burning Texas sky. The two trees in the backyard and one in the front towered over our home with a kind of regal elegance and regularly bore buttery nuts in the late spring.

In 2005, they turned strange, however. All summer long, they began losing limbs, in some instances at a wild, feverish pace. Thick, scaly branches ripped away, cracking the air with a screeching sound, then plummeted noiselessly to the ground. All down my block, branches crashed on top of cars and roofs and lawns, yielding a great whine of chainsaws.

Good things that should have been strong and enduring were falling apart.

Much the same can be said about this past year: marriages broken by infidelity; families torn apart by political animosities; congregations damaged and then fractured by the abuse of authority; cities roiled by cycles of protest and counterprotest, some of them turning brutally violent; landscapes ravaged by fires.

Seeing so many things break down in the world around us can cause even the sturdiest among us to begin to lose it. We lose hope. We lose the will to care. And when left to our own devices, dark despair settles in and corrodes our senses of what's real and good and worthwhile.

This is where the words of the prophet Isaiah speak to us across the centuries to convey a word of hope. "Hold on, dear pilgrim," he tells us. "Hold on." Then the Lord speaks in Isaiah 35:3–4:

> Strengthen the feeble hands,
> steady the knees that give way;
> say to those with fearful hearts,
> "Be strong, do not fear."

Blind, deaf, lame, and mute—of both body and heart—will be made whole. Wastelands will blossom. The hot sands will become a cool oasis. Wrongs will be made right, and the redeemed will return home dancing with halos of everlasting joy. It will not always be dark and dreadful.

When things in our lives and the world around us keep falling apart, in ways that might seem utterly pointless or downright merciless, it's easy to lose hope. And when we lose hope, the world can feel terribly bleak and not worth bothering about.

God knows our hearts need help in such times. He knows our hands will grow weak and our hearts fearful. He knows we'll want to give up, even if only in small ways. So, it is to us, here and now, that he speaks a word of promise: "Gladness and joy will overtake [you], and sorrow and sighing will flee away" (v. 10).

We lost one of the pecan trees at our old Austin home, and the two that remained looked haggard and spindly. I imagine many of us feel similarly today. We feel worn down by all the things that are breaking down. But to each of us, our Lord speaks: "Be strong, and do not be afraid. I am coming. I am coming and will set all things right."

SEEING SO MANY THINGS BREAK DOWN IN THE WORLD AROUND US CAN CAUSE EVEN THE STURDIEST AMONG US TO BEGIN TO LOSE IT.

DIRTY FRANK

E.M. WELCHER

is the pastor of Grace Baptist Church in Vermillion, South Dakota. He is the author of *Advent: A Thread in the Night*, *Nightscapes: Poems from the Depths*, and *Resplendent Bride: Essays on Love and Loss*. Find him on Substack.

When I was in my 20s, my brother gave me his dog. Professor Frank. Eighty-five pounds of black-and-white stray mutt. Red collar.

His tail, a cedar of Lebanon, thumped against walls, shins, the very world itself, and your soul. But his heart weighed 99 pounds. His love reverberated through the plywood of the mobile home I rented, *thump, thump, thump*, like the heart of God pulsing through redemptive history.

We would cruise around the sacred hills and hollows in my black Ford F-250. Then we picked out a house. Frank slept in the mudroom. His tail gave a pulse to our home.

I met a girl. Frank thought she was sure neato keen. We got married. She died.

A man has a way of turning in on himself. All the hues of the day simmer down to nothing much worth watching, so you stare at the wall a bit. Shadows lengthen, but you don't bother turning the light on. The garbage has more bottles in it than you care to admit, and perhaps you catch a glimpse of yourself in your truck window and realize the bags beneath your eyes reveal that the rhetoric of faith seldom pans out into gold. Maybe you turn on a show to ignore. I merely sat and watched reruns in my head, with no love left to give.

The pulse of the house went quiet. Behemoth's tail failed to wag in the mudroom. I went to see the mutt, and he barely bothered to look up. The dog missed her too. He mourned with a broken heart. Nothing's sadder than a brokenhearted dog.

I lay prostrate on the unswept mudroom floor, like I was at one of those churches where you let everybody know you're about to get serious with the praying. I lay down next to my mutt friend, petted him for a while, and finally said, "I miss her too, boy."

Like a dead man shocked back to the land of the living, I heard the house's pulse resume, *thump, thump, thump*, as Frank's tail returned to life.

Sometimes all we need to start inching away from the darkness is an acknowledgment of the wreckage. "Oh, I see there's parts of you all over the highway, and your heart is nowhere to be found." The wreckage has gone beyond the repair of human hands, but the cognizance goes a long way.

I suppose that's why the prophet Isaiah let us all know that the Christ would be "a man of sorrows and acquainted with grief" (53:3, ESV).

The Lord Jesus is a wild man. He sent prophet after prophet to Jerusalem—even showed up himself to gather his people as a hen gathers her chicks beneath her wings. But they would not have it (Matt. 23:37).

He sent me a dog.

SOMETIMES ALL WE NEED
TO START INCHING AWAY
FROM THE DARKNESS IS
AN ACKNOWLEDGMENT
OF THE WRECKAGE.

W1 | D6

LIVING IN THE DARK SPACE

HEATHER THOMPSON DAY

is the author of *What If I'm Wrong?* and host of the *What If I'm Wrong?* podcast.

I was watching my son come out of the water at the beach. He was laughing until he wasn't. He couldn't see me. I watched him scan the sand for my chair.

"Mom!" he shouted while starting to panic. He thought he was lost because he couldn't see me. But he wasn't lost at all. He had stopped watching me, but I never stopped watching him.

I have gone through dark spaces in my life. Gaps where I couldn't see how the dots would connect where I was with where I hoped to be going. I have shouted at the ceiling. I have prayed into the darkness. I have cried out to a God that I couldn't see anymore. These gaps are what I call "dark spaces." They're the spaces between what we see and what we can't. Between faith and fear. Uncertainty and urgency. Hope and hallucinations.

Dark spaces are inevitable. The word *darkness* is used around 150 times in the Bible. On earth there will be darkness. But there will also be light. Much of life is spent navigating the gap in between. It's a theme of Scripture—the ongoing battle between darkness and light. None of us will escape it.

I want my obedience to God to come with a detailed prophecy of how these stars align. I want a visible string. Thread the needle and show me the yarn. But so rarely does what I want match what I have experienced. And we don't talk about the dark spaces enough.

The dark space between "I surrender all" and "once I see how it turns out." Between singleness and the altar. Between the womb and the baby. Between the diagnosis and the healing. Between the last two weeks' pay and the new-hire form. Between the moving and the landing.

The hardest part of faith is standing ten toes deep in the gaps of these dark spaces. It feels like quicksand, like your knees will disappear while praying on them. Yet Scripture is filled with dark spaces. And very few of our heroes managed them well. Job nearly died in his descent into the dark space. Sarah laughed in hers. Hannah wept in the bitterness of it. And Jonah ran from his.

Jesus was born to secure the gap between Eden and our eternity in heaven. There will be no more waiting then. No more quicksand. No more "Where is God?" or "I can't see you." God came to earth to stand ten toes deep with us in the dark spaces.

"I thought I'd see you by now," I cried out to God in my bedroom one evening. And that's when I remembered the beach. My son thought he had been lost. But he wasn't lost at all. He had stopped watching me, but I never stopped watching him.

So it is with God every time we step into the darkness. There is a Light that sees you, even when you can't see it.

THE HARDEST PART OF FAITH
IS STANDING TEN TOES DEEP IN THE
GAPS OF THESE DARK SPACES.

W1|D7

FROM LIMPING TO LEAPING

JARED C. WILSON

is pastor for preaching at Liberty Baptist Church in Liberty, Missouri, and assistant professor of pastoral ministry at Midwestern Seminary in Kansas City, Missouri. He is the author of over 20 books, including *Friendship with the Friend of Sinners* and *Lest We Drift*.

"Look, the day is coming, burning like a furnace, when all the arrogant and everyone who commits wickedness will become stubble. The coming day will consume them,' says the Lord of Armies, 'not leaving them root or branches. But for you who fear my name, the sun of righteousness will rise with healing in its wings, and you will go out and playfully jump like calves from the stall'" (Mal. 4:1–2, CSB).

"Jared, have you ever seen calves jumping?"

"No, I don't think I have," I replied.

It was a bitterly cold, late November day in Vermont, and I sat at the bedside of my friend Natalie, who was bundled up under layers of blankets. Natalie was dying of pancreatic cancer. Much earlier in the year, the doctors had given her a matter of weeks to live, but she'd outlived their predictions. Feeble and frail, she was now spending her final days in the home of her best friends, where they'd set up hospice in a basement apartment. I was Natalie's pastor and had visited her each week, spending substantial time praying and reading Scripture with her and listening to her reflect on life, death, and everything in between. Christmas was coming, and barring a miracle, it would be her last.

Natalie had unusual requests for Scripture readings. She would become preoccupied with particular passages in the Bible, wanting me to read them to her every time I visited, for weeks on end. We'd read John 10 and Revelation 1–3 over and over again. Now we were multiple days into Malachi chapter 4. And no, I'd never seen calves jumping.

When we'd been neck-deep in John 10, Natalie had described the behavior of sheep who recognize their shepherd's voice. Now she was telling me that when calves are figuring out what their bodies do, they bounce across the pasture in ways you wouldn't expect.

I said, "I see." But I really didn't. I was having a hard time picturing it, perhaps because I didn't have the capacity at the time to visualize such an image of joy. My friend was dying. And she wasn't the first. We'd seen so much death in our little country church. I'd lost numerous friends to cancer—young parents, people I'd baptized, people I cared about deeply. Natalie was an older woman but had otherwise been very healthy. She was definitely going "before her time." And as it seemed I'd spent the last three years of ministry largely in hospitals, at bedsides, and in funeral parlors, I was worn out. I didn't feel like leaping. But Natalie did.

As painful as life had become for her, she just kept talking about seeing Jesus. Everyone else was preparing for Christmas, when Jesus came to us. She was preparing for heaven and going to him. We talked about the glory of that moment. We talked about the glories of the new earth to come, when these bodies that we can't keep from winding down finally give way to bodies that won't decay and will live forever. By God's grace, it wasn't just those blankets keeping Natalie warm; it was her hope in Malachi 4:2's "sun of righteousness." Her healing was coming.

THESE BODIES THAT WE CAN'T KEEP FROM WINDING DOWN FINALLY GIVE WAY TO BODIES THAT WON'T DECAY AND WILL LIVE FOREVER.

Christmas came. My family and I traveled back home to Texas, but we returned to Vermont the week after. I hadn't seen Natalie in a couple of weeks, so after settling in, I drove over to the basement apartment to visit her.

It was January 1. I didn't know—no one had told me—but Natalie had died that morning. I arrived just as her husband and a few others were navigating bringing the pine box she requested as her casket down the staircase. I didn't get to say goodbye.

Her memorial service was held in the spring. As I sat at the big picture window in our rural home, trying to figure out my funeral sermon, I glanced out at the hillside across the street. And there to my surprise and delight came a calf, bounding exuberantly across the rocky hill. I couldn't believe it! It was a hilarious, adorable, joyful sight. Now I knew what Natalie knew.

And one day I will know what Natalie knows—that as dark as our Christmases may be, the sun of righteousness will rise with healing in its wings. The first time, Christ came to die. But he rose from his grave. He will come to us again. The lame hearts of those who trust in him will leap in their chests. And all will be well.

WEEK 1

REFLECTION

LIGHT DAWNS IN THE DARKNESS
FOR THE UPRIGHT; HE IS GRACIOUS,
MERCIFUL, AND RIGHTEOUS.

PSALM 112:4, ESV

As you begin this Advent season, take a few minutes to reflect on how you are coming into it. Do you feel excited and hopeful as the days unfold around you? Are you experiencing anxiety due to pressures and expectations being laid on you? Maybe you have some deep loneliness, a physical issue, or an unresolved relationship conflict. Take a moment to lay your hopes and heartaches at the feet of Christ.

What is one story in particular that stuck out to you during this week's readings? In what ways does it help you apply the grace and mercy of Jesus to your own story?

Advent, which means "arrival," carries a sense of longing and anticipation for what is to come. What is something that you are longing for and anticipating this month? How does the birth of Christ ultimately fill our greatest longing?

WEEK 2

[Christmas] means not just hope for the world, despite all its unending problems, but hope for you and me, despite all our unending failings.

TIM KELLER

The people who walked in darkness have seen a great light; those who dwelt in a land of deep darkness, on them has light shone.

ISAIAH 9:2

ESV

W2|D1

HELD TOGETHER BY A CORNERSTONE

J. A. MEDDERS

(PhD) is the director of theology and content for Send Network and the general editor for New Churches. He also writes regularly at SpiritualTheology.net and hosts the *Home Row* podcast for writers.

Rubble was everywhere. Over a decade of life in a local church was lost in a conflict. Deep roots severed. Old friendships went up in flames. The explosion sent shock waves through home after home. Shrapnel left me with a limp. And that's not the worst of it.

Anxiety and depression took the spare bedroom. And they were terrible guests—awful in every way you can imagine. They were annoying when I needed peace, quiet, and rest. They were crippling when I wanted to do something—anything. They started making themselves at home, spilling out of the guest room and redecorating the house according to their style and vibe. It's darker than you realize. Funhouse mirrors are a favorite accent. They paint the walls a dark shade of contorted reality. And while they don't know plumbing or electrical, it doesn't stop them from tinkering. Thankfully, they couldn't harm the foundation of the house.

The foundation stands.

People see my nearly smooth scars now and ask, "Why didn't you deconstruct? What kept you from leaving Christianity? And why, after everything you've been through, do you still serve the church?" Serious questions deserve sincere consideration.

The answer is as clear and serious as the noonday sun: because Jesus is real.

The incarnate Son of God, Jesus Christ, is our foundation. Christmas is no myth. It's not a cute story. The validity of Christianity is not based on our experiences; it's based on him and his Word.

The eternal Son of God really did come to earth from another realm to save us. He was actually placed in Mary's womb by the power of the Holy Spirit to be our redeemer. Fully God and fully man, Jesus was born in Bethlehem. He came to die for our sins (Gal. 3:13), to destroy the works of the devil (1 John 3:8), and to rise for our right standing before God (Rom. 4:25). And he really is building his church with himself as the foundation (Eph. 2:20). It's all true. I must follow him.

The foundation—the cornerstone—is dependable. You can trust him. Isaiah tells us that this is "a tested stone, a precious cornerstone, a sure foundation; the one who believes will be unshakable" (28:16, CSB). Jesus is acquainted with our griefs (53:3). He knows heartache and suffering more than anyone. The stone went through a stress test, and he passed.

When your house is built on Christ and his Word, you are unshakable (Matt. 7:24–25). The storms will come. You will sway in the wind, and you will be beaten by the rain. A new roof, walls, and flooring may be needed—but the foundation holds. You are held fast in him. As the old hymn tells us, "When all around my soul gives way, he then is all my hope and stay." Christmas is the story of the delivery and installation of your cornerstone, your hope and stay.

As I sat in the rubble, new friends helped me realize where I was sitting. Christ was always holding me up. Rest and rejoice in him, your firm foundation.

CHRISTMAS IS NO MYTH.
IT'S NOT A CUTE STORY.
THE VALIDITY OF CHRISTIANITY
IS NOT BASED ON OUR
EXPERIENCES; IT'S BASED ON
HIM AND HIS WORD.

W2|D2

THESE DARK DAYS

JEREMY WRITEBOL

is the lead campus pastor of Woodside Bible Church in Plymouth, Michigan, and the executive director of Gospel-Centered Discipleship. He is the author of several books including *Make It Your Ambition*, the award-winning *Pastor, Jesus Is Enough*, and *everPresent: How the Gospel Relocates Us in the Present*.

The darkness haunts me. During the successive weeks of Advent, I want the mood to lift, the light to shine, and the joy to radiate. Yet the illuminated tree, songs of good tidings and cheer, sweet cookies, and all the trimmings of "the most wonderful time of the year" can't overcome the foreboding darkness that looms just on the other side of December 25.

As I meander further into my middle-aged years, the fear of greater hardship and affliction grows. December 25 gives way not to bliss and joy but to the literal darkness of January. Short daylight hours, bone-chilling cold, and the slog of a new year of work bring me into a depressive state. Another page of the calendar turns, and my concerns multiply. Will this be the year everything goes so poorly that I'm ruined? Will the world break apart in an all-out war? Will I be so short-sighted and uncaring that I make an irredeemable mess? Is this the year the other shoe drops and grief shrouds my eyes from any joy?

Left to my own ruminations, the darkness wins. Every time. My perspective is too narrow and jaded to gain a glimpse over the horizon. The darkness is too pervasive to think a dawning light could drive the shadows away. Hope is for those who are already winners.

That is, of course, if you ignore God's promise. The promise.

The promise isn't for the winners. It's not for the whole and healthy or the rich and powerful. The promise is for

W2|D2

those who live in the land of deep darkness. "*On them* has light shone" (Isa. 9:2, ESV, emphasis mine). Embracing that promise takes a mountain, or only a mustard seed, of humility. I live in that dark land. I am both a creation and a creator of it. Yet if I admit that the darkness dwells within me, I am poised to be on the receiving end of the promise.

The light has shone. Jesus confronts our present darkness with his piercing light: "While I am in the world, I am the light of the world" (John 9:5). He comforts fearful and cowering dwellers of the darkness, saying, "Do not let your hearts be troubled. You believe in God; believe also in me" (14:1). He delivers us from the dominion of darkness, bringing us into his kingdom through the shedding of his own blood (Col. 1:13).

The light will shine. The present darkness does not stand a chance with the coming Second Advent. Jesus is "the radiance of God's glory" (Heb. 1:3). When he comes again, he will put all things to rights. His light of grace and justice will fully illuminate even the secret things. It's by his glorious light that the nations will walk. Darkness will not overcome, "for the Lord God will give them light. And they will reign for ever and ever" (Rev. 22:5).

Yes, darkness is present. The darkness may get deeper still. But the promise is dawning. *Post tenebras lux*. "After darkness, light."

THE PROMISE IS FOR THOSE
WHO LIVE IN THE LAND
OF DEEP DARKNESS.

W2|D3

SO SHALL IT BE

JONAH SAGE

serves as one of the pastors of Sojourn Church in New Albany, Indiana. He completed his undergraduate studies in philosophy at Miami University (Oxford, Ohio) and received his master of divinity from The Southern Baptist Theological Seminary in 2013.

When the ultrasound tech said, "Sit tight. The doctor will be in shortly," she had enough "uh-oh" in her voice to tell us something wasn't right. Our normal ob-gyn was away (of course), so a stranger sat before us holding pictures of my daughter's brain. After pointing out six "cloudy spots" on the scan, he explained two scenarios. In the first, these cysts would result in the death of our daughter sometime before her first birthday. In the second, she would be fine. "She's fine or she isn't," he said. The only test available endangered her life, so the doctor asked us how to proceed. I stared at this man's degrees on the wall, wondering how this could be our decision to make. We chose life and the ambiguity of anxious waiting.

Normal life continued. Fall transitioned into Advent. I watched my full-term wife show my infant son how to arrange our Dickens' Village houses just right. We decorated the tree. We wrapped a baby doll for him to open on Christmas morning, hoping it would teach him to be gentle with his sister who may or may not come home. The waiting—that awful mix of hope and horror—carried us into the new year. The regular rhythms of ministry ticked by like the heart monitors of congregants I visited at the hospital. I rehearsed the statistics provided by the doctors. *She's fine. It's fine.* We waited.

Advent turned to Christmas and then Epiphany. We feasted with our church family. We prepared for Lent. We

W2|D3

faced the whiplash of seemingly contradictory emotions embedded in the church calendar.

The night before Ash Wednesday, a once-in-a-decade blizzard descended on Louisville. We gathered the next day, with snow burying the world around us, to remember we were dying. I wondered if my daughter was still living.

On February 18, 2015, at roughly 6:40 a.m., my phone began vibrating during my homily. I read the message: "She's coming." We barreled through the snow to the hospital. Tears exploded when the doctor, playing a perfect Rafiki, lifted my daughter into the air.

"Is she okay?" I choked out. She was beautiful. She was healthy. She was perfect. In the twinkling of an eye, terror transformed into joy.

Our waiting taught us something of how to wait and of what is awaiting us when the waiting is over. Ours is no longer an ambiguous waiting. It may at times be painful and persistent, but it is neither vain nor uncertain. We know that when we see Jesus, we will be made like him. No one whose hope is in the Lord is ever put to shame, so we face our waiting, complicated and unpleasant as it may be. We hold our contradictory emotions. We rest in the goodness of him who keeps all his promises. He promised a child would be born unto us, and so he was. That child promised that new life would be born in each of us, and so shall it be.

OURS IS NO LONGER AN
AMBIGUOUS WAITING.
IT MAY AT TIMES BE
PAINFUL AND PERSISTENT,
BUT IT IS NEITHER VAIN
NOR UNCERTAIN.

BEND TOWARD THE LIGHT

JONATHAN HOLMES

is the executive director of Fieldstone Counseling and the interim executive director of Christian Counseling & Educational Foundation (CCEF). He also serves as an instructor at Westminster Theological Seminary in the master of arts in counseling program.

I've been told that during and after COVID-19, many of us picked up a variety of hobbies—from sourdough-bread making to new workout routines and regimens, we all tried to find something to help us pass the time. For me, it was plants; what started with a solo pothos plant from Lowe's on an ignored shelf became a burgeoning collection of all manner of plants. Confession: I have killed many a plant in my brief career, but I've come to understand that one absolutely essential element for all plants is good lighting. Light is king in the plant world.

Because of this reality, one of the hardest times for a plant lover like myself is the winter; the days and sunlit hours are shorter, and the nights are long and cold, especially here in the Midwest. A few days ago, I came into my kitchen and saw that several of my plants were looking a bit sad and depressed. Yet a slice of sunshine was coming through the windows that was particularly bright for even this cold day. I'm sure it could have been my imagination, but it seemed that one of the plants was bending toward the light, as if crying out, "I can't take this dreariness forever. I must get to you."

It was a stark reminder that we share some similarities with plants. That shouldn't surprise us at all. Botanical and arboreal themes abound throughout Scripture. Like plants, we humans aren't made for the darkness. We don't thrive there. But, for whatever reason, we often find

W2|D4

ourselves there. Whether by choice or circumstance, every human being experiences dark times and days.

What darkness envelops you today? Perhaps it's the long winter months we find ourselves in, the overwhelming expectations of the holiday season, the pain and heartbreak of broken and estranged relationships—we've all been there. Darkness is defined by the absence of light. In the dark, we can feel abandoned, forgotten, and unloved.

What are we to do, then? Like my plant, we do whatever we can to bend toward the Light. The prophet Jeremiah seems to capture this aching tension of living in the reality of a broken, dark world but also straining for whatever ray of light we can faithfully see: "The Lord will not cast off forever, for, though he cause grief, he will have compassion according to the abundance of his steadfast love; for he does not afflict from his heart or grieve the children of men" (Lam. 3:31–33, ESV).

In times of darkness, my encouragement to my own heart and yours today is to do whatever it takes to bend toward the Light. Bending our hearts toward Jesus is an act of faith, because sometimes the darkness feels so overwhelming to us. But we remind ourselves and others that it's in the light that we truly flourish. As the apostle John records in relation to Christ's first advent, "The true light that gives light to everyone was coming into the world" (John 1:9).

IN TIMES OF DARKNESS, MY ENCOURAGEMENT TO MY OWN HEART AND YOURS TODAY IS TO DO WHATEVER IT TAKES TO BEND TOWARD THE LIGHT.

W2|D5

NO MORE NIGHT

JONATHAN K. DODSON

has served as the founding pastor of City Life Church, a theologian in residence, and the founder of the resource ministry Gospel-Centered Discipleship. He is married to his remarkable wife, Robie, and is the author of numerous books, including *The Unwavering Pastor*.

One day we noticed that the trim around our door frames was especially dark. I assumed we hadn't dusted enough. Then we noticed discoloration on the concrete floors, and it hit us—there's mold in the house! This led to major upheaval in our lives. Then, within weeks, financial investments bottomed out, my wife was in a car accident, and I lost my job.

We struggled with anxiety about finances, worry that we would lose our home, and a sense of injustice. But mostly, we were sad. It felt like we were in the pitch black of night. When our pastor asked my daughter how she was handling everything, she replied, "We are grieving. We also know that sometimes you have to sacrifice things for the spread of the gospel. But we're also sad."

It's important to hold both of these realities in tension: grief over loss and hope in gospel gain. If we just brandish our hope, we won't experience the deep comfort of releasing our sorrows to the suffering Savior. But if we get mired in our grief, without a sense of what God is doing, we will spin out into despair.

In Revelation 21, John writes about our future with great hope: "The city does not need the sun or the moon to shine on it, for the glory of God gives it light, and the Lamb is its lamp. The nations will walk by its light, and the kings of the earth will bring their splendor into it. On no day will its gates ever be shut, for there will be no night there" (vv. 23–25).

W2|D5

Within this stunning description of life under the unwaning sun of God's glory is a hint of previous darkness: "and there will be no night there." In this brief phrase, John acknowledges the unwelcome darkness of suffering. Earlier he describes God's judgment wiping out a third of all lights in the sky (8:12). The exiled apostle writes about the glory of Christ with a profound sense of how dark things can get. Yet he knows the night is on notice.

One day, there will be no more night. Life will be so peaceful and safe that the protective gates of the city will never need closing. There will be no threat of loss, no pain of grief, no more injustice. Only light.

The good news is that light can break into our lives now. Jesus' undiminished glory illuminates our present path like a shaft of light in the darkness. If we trust him with our heartaches and step out to follow him, he will lead us into the light of the eternal city. While this doesn't immediately resolve the tension between grief and hope, it does diminish the darkness of night.

Another daughter had strep and was confined to the house for several days. Toward the end of the week, we decided to go outside together. As we stepped out into the warm sunlight, she said, "Daddy, the light hurts."

I replied, "That's because you've been in the dark so long. Once you get used to the light, you'll see it's a beautiful day."

Coming out of the darkness can be painful, even scary, but as we step into the light, our eyes adjust to take in the brilliance of Jesus, who brings us unique comfort and hope.

THE EXILED APOSTLE WRITES
ABOUT THE GLORY OF CHRIST WITH
A PROFOUND SENSE OF HOW DARK
THINGS CAN GET. YET HE KNOWS
THE NIGHT IS ON NOTICE.

W2 | D6

AN INVITATION TO BELIEVE

BARNABAS PIPER

is a pastor at Immanuel Church in Nashville, Tennessee. He is the author of several books, including *Help My Unbelief* and *Belong*. He is married to Lauren and has three children.

When I was 27, my faith fell apart. To be more accurate, the house of cards I had carefully constructed to look like faith fell apart.

For years I had hidden certain doubts and hypocrisies behind theological knowledge and articulate arguments. I gave the impression of confidence in Christ while actually grasping at confidence in myself. And then it all blew up. I was fired from a job for dishonesty and theft. My sin was exposed, and the damage it caused was deep. Worst of all, though, I was forced to confront the question "What do you actually believe?" Not "What do you profess?" or "What do you assent to?" but "What do you stake your life on?"

And I couldn't very well answer. All my previous professions of faith had brought me to this place. I was staring into the chasm of unbelief, on the brink of falling in completely, and realizing I didn't know how to believe or whom to believe in.

Amid this crisis, an elder from my church who was patiently caring for me and offering guidance urged, "Go back and read the Gospels and look for Jesus. Try to forget all your preconceptions." That's not an easy thing for a pastor's kid, Sunday schooler, sword-drill champion, memory-verse A-lister, Bible trivia ace, and flannelgraph aficionado. Preconceptions were, in many ways, all I had.

But I did my best. Starting in Matthew 1, I read stories and passages I'd read a hundred times. I read through Jesus'

W2|D6

teachings and about his miracles. I muddled and trudged my way into Mark. Then I got to Mark 9 and the account of a desperate father bringing his demon-possessed son to Jesus for deliverance. I knew this story. It barely registered as significant in the moment, except for one interaction:

> "It has often cast him into fire and into water, to destroy him. But if you can do anything, have compassion on us and help us." And Jesus said to him, "'If you can'! All things are possible for one who believes." Immediately the father of the child cried out and said, "I believe; help my unbelief!" (Mark 9:22–24, ESV)

This grabbed my attention. When a struggling doubter brought those doubts to Jesus and asked for help, Jesus didn't reject or condemn him for his struggles. The man could look Jesus in the face and say, "Help my unbelief" and Jesus would. This offered a paradigm for real faith: belief with struggle, belief with dependence.

The words I had so often skipped over began to take on flesh in the living person and reality of Jesus. Whereas I had been unmoved by reading of Jesus' birth, I now discovered another sort of advent—when Jesus comes alive in a soul.

These discoveries weren't immediate. Yet seeing those verses that day was the spark that caught the tinder of my heart. Over the ensuing months, the flame flickered, then crackled, then roared into heat and light in my heart. Jesus invited me into belief and showed me he is indeed the life who is the light for men's hearts (John 1:4).

WHEN A STRUGGLING DOUBTER
BROUGHT THOSE DOUBTS TO JESUS
AND ASKED FOR HELP,
JESUS DIDN'T REJECT OR CONDEMN
HIM FOR HIS STRUGGLES.

W2 | D7

HOPE THAT CANNOT BE OVERSHADOWED

CHRIS JONES

is the founding and lead pastor of Redeemer Community Church in Bloomington, Indiana. He's been married to his wife, Krystal, for 25 years, and they have three children.

Summer of 2022 was a high point in my life. I was on sabbatical, getting some much-needed rest and an abundance of quality time with my family and the Lord. Psalm 16:5–6 became the theme of that season: "Lord, you are my portion and my cup of blessing; you hold my future. The boundary lines have fallen for me in pleasant places; indeed, I have a beautiful inheritance" (CSB). The Lord was helping me embrace my limitations and see his goodness in both the highs and lows of life and ministry. I returned from that season of rest with renewed hope and joy in the provision and promises of God in my life.

But immediately upon my return, it was all put to the test. The hopeful light of that season was replaced with discouraging darkness. My first day back as lead pastor came with the news that a staff member was preparing to leave. This was followed by the departures of several church members, leaving a wake of grief and pain. It was a season of discouragement unlike any other I had experienced in my years of pastoring.

Aside from the ministry pains, my wife was bearing the weight of caring for her father, who was suffering from dementia. Together, we shared the burden of praying for our oldest son, who remained close to our family but had distanced himself from the church and his faith a couple years before. We found ourselves facing so many discouragements

W2|D7

and challenges. By November, it felt like all the light of the summer was on the verge of being overshadowed.

But then the season of Advent came with the reminder "The light shines in the darkness, and the darkness has not overcome it" (John 1:5). This is one of the great gifts this season presents to us. It invites us to remember that no matter how dark things might seem, light has come and is coming again, and darkness cannot overcome it. Advent bade me to not forget the lessons of the summer and to embrace that even amid discouragement, the boundary lines have fallen for me in pleasant places, the Lord holds my future, and I still have a beautiful inheritance.

Jesus was so good in that season to lead me to cling to him and the hope he brings, even if it meant waiting for things to actually feel hopeful. And he was gracious to not make us wait too long. Within a few months, a spirit of joyful hope returned to our church. Even more beautifully, the Lord brought our son to faith in one of the most amazing transformations I have seen.

Whatever you are facing in this season, however dark things might seem, remember that light has come and is coming again, and darkness cannot and will never overcome it. The beautiful inheritance we have in Christ cannot be overshadowed.

NO MATTER HOW DARK
THINGS MIGHT SEEM,
LIGHT HAS COME
AND IS COMING AGAIN,
AND DARKNESS CANNOT
OVERCOME IT.

WEEK 2

REFLECTION

THE PEOPLE WHO WALKED IN DARKNESS HAVE SEEN A GREAT LIGHT; THOSE WHO DWELT IN A LAND OF DEEP DARKNESS, ON THEM HAS LIGHT SHONE.

ISAIAH 9:2, ESV

Take a moment to reflect on God's unfolding plan of redemption that began in the garden and led to the manger. What does this story of redemption tell us about the nature and character of God? What are some attributes of God that you need him to illuminate in your life during this season?

What is one story in particular that stuck out to you during this week's readings? As you read other people's stories of darkness and light, what does it uniquely highlight in your own story?

Christmastime has a way of amplifying some of the difficult things we experience in our day-to-day lives. What is one truth you need reminding of today that might help redirect your hope back to the promises of Christ? Who could you encourage with this hope?

WEEK 3

The Christmas message is that there is hope for a ruined humanity—hope of pardon, hope of peace with God, hope of glory—because at the Father's will Jesus Christ became poor and was born in a stable so that thirty years later he might hang on a cross.

J.I. PACKER

If I say, "Surely the darkness shall cover me, and the light about me be night," even the darkness is not dark to you; the night is bright as the day, for darkness is as light with you.

PSALM 139:11-12

ESV

W3|D1

THE STORM AND THE PROMISE

AARON ARMSTRONG

is the author of *Faith Simplified: What We Believe and Why We Believe It*. For nearly 20 years, he has served local churches as a preacher, small-group leader, and children's ministry leader.

"Mom passed away this afternoon." My sister-in-law spoke the five words no one wants to hear—especially not on Christmas Eve. As we adults talked quietly on the phone, our kids half watched a Christmas movie and ate their dinner, trying to figure out what was going on.

It was Chinese takeout, our family's yearslong Christmas Eve tradition. It was cold before we grown-ups took a bite.

We walked in circles outside, reeling. We'd experienced death in our extended family before, but this was different. This was my wife Emily's mother. This was the first of our parents to die. Even as we tried to process the news and planned to get Emily to Canada to be with her dad and sister, Christmas loomed large. What would the next day be like? How would we tell our friends—our gospel family here in Tennessee—about what happened without ruining their Christmas?

The next day was heavy but normal. Presents, food, and another failed attempt at rallying the family around a reading of the birth of Jesus (Luke 2:1–20). Phone calls and texts with family. Quiet time to contemplate.

The following days and weeks were a blur of calls, texts, tears, and travel. As January passed into February, we prayed for a sense of normalcy. We didn't yet know this was only the beginning of a storm that would rage for over a year: A major health scare and surgery. Another unexpected death, this time my sister's husband, a man I'd known for over 30 years. The end of our church of more than eight years.

We prayed for the storm to end and for peace to come. But instead of Jesus calming the storm (Mark 4:39), our boat was overturned. Instead of finding stillness, we were washed up on the shore to sit beside Job, the weary saint who helped me see the light.

It's easy to misread Job's story, especially when God breaks his silence and responds to Job's complaints (Job 38–40). His "Where were you when" stings, seeming to say, "I'm God. You're not. So how about you sit down and shut your mouth?" Yet one small but important detail challenges this idea: "Then the Lord spoke to Job out of the storm" (38:1). When God appears, he is identified by his intimate, covenantal name—YHWH, I Am Who I Am. The name given to sustain his people in their distress (Ex. 3:14). The name that told them he was with them in their trials—and tells us the same.

He is with us in the storm.

That is Advent's promise, one Christ's birth made manifest as "the Word became flesh and made his dwelling among us" (John 1:14). Despair will haunt us, but God will not abandon us. Storms will come, but Christ is with us. Darkness will come, but after darkness comes light.

And one year later, on Christmas Eve, we sat down for dinner. It was Chinese takeout, our family's yearslong tradition. It was hot when we took our first bite.

DESPAIR WILL HAUNT US,
BUT GOD WILL NOT ABANDON US.
STORMS WILL COME,
BUT CHRIST IS WITH US.

W3|D2

DARKNESS TO LIGHT

MALCOLM GUITE

is a poet-priest who lectures widely in England and North America on theology and literature and has published various books on poetry, theology, and literary criticism.

"The people walking in darkness have seen a great light." Those prophetic words of Isaiah 9:2 continue to have a powerful resonance for us today. They came true supremely, for the whole world, at Christmas when Christ the Light of the World was born for us in a stable. But they also come true for us time and again in our individual lives when, at times seemingly against all odds, the light of Christ shines anew for us.

I am someone who occasionally experiences the real darkness of depression. Often there seems to be no outward reason for it. It is as though the light in my world suddenly dims or goes out altogether, and I feel that I am stumbling in the dark—or worse, not even stumbling; I can hardly get out of bed or even breathe. But I hold on. I "keep on keeping on," as Bob Dylan says, and I pray through clenched teeth.

I wrote about that experience once in an Advent poem about Isaiah's promises that Christ would be given "the key to the house of David" (22:22) and set the prisoners free (61:1):

> Even in the darkness where I sit
> And huddle in the midst of misery
> I can remember freedom, but forget
> That every lock must answer to a key.

W3|D2

I go on to confess in that poem:

> I cry out for the key I threw away
> That turned and over turned with certain touch
> And with the lovely lifting of a latch
> Opened my darkness to the light of day.

And he does come. After I wrote that poem, the darkness began to lift a little. By way of recovery, I went and stayed a few days on the little sailboat I kept on the River Orwell, on the east coast of England. After a night on the boat, I got up very early in the morning and stood on the foredeck to watch the sun rise over the river. I recited the ancient Advent Antiphon prayer "O Oriens" (O Dayspring), which goes like this:

O Dayspring, splendor of light eternal and sun of righteousness:
Come and enlighten those who dwell in darkness and the shadow of death.

As the sun rose and I watched the path of its light on the river, my prayer was answered and my inner darkness lifted completely. I celebrated that in another sonnet:

> First light and then first lines along the east
> To touch and brush a sheen of light on water,
> As though behind the sky itself they traced
> The shift and shimmer of another river . . .
> So every trace of light begins a grace

AT TIMES SEEMINGLY AGAINST ALL ODDS, THE LIGHT OF CHRIST SHINES ANEW FOR US.

In me, a beckoning. The smallest gleam
Is somehow a beginning and a calling;
"Sleeper awake, the darkness was a dream
For you will see the Dayspring at your waking,
Beyond your long last line the dawn is breaking."

(Poems from *Sounding the Seasons*, Canterbury Press, 2012, pp. 10–11)

W3|D3

GOD OF LIGHT AND LIFE

MATTHEW Z. CAPPS

(MDiv, DMin, PhD candidate) serves as the lead pastor of Fairview Baptist Church in Apex, North Carolina. Matt is the author of *Drawn by Beauty* and *Every Member Matters*.

The summer before my freshman year of high school, I traveled on my first mission trip to New York City to assist several church plants, pray for people on the streets, and share the gospel with people in the park. It was a challenging but fruitful week. I fondly remember getting on my knees and "giving my life to the work of ministry" during our last evening of worship at the Marriott World Trade Center, nestled between the Twin Towers.

It should not surprise us that the Evil One, personal sin, and the world's pleasures increase their temptation after a spiritual high like I experienced that summer. Indeed, after I entered high school, those moments of service and surrender faded as I was enveloped in my new surroundings. From that point, the lure of a life untethered to a Christian family and the local church led me to move four hours away to attend university. There, unrestrained and intoxicated living brought me to a place of nihilism and hopelessness. Looking back, I realize I spent most of my high school and college years fumbling in the darkness, spiritually empty and aimless.

Then came the morning of September 11, 2001. All of us who experienced it remember where we were on that day of darkness in our country. The unprecedented events surrounding that fateful day brought our nation to its knees. Yet God used that national tragedy to wake me from personal darkness. You see, I was brought to my knees as well.

W3 D3

As I sat alone in my dorm room watching the second plane crash into the South Tower, I could not help but think about that summer before high school. While I watched the towers fall, by God's grace I could not help but question my trajectory and the inevitable end of my future. Just five years earlier, I had been in those very buildings. On a mission trip. Surrendering my life to gospel ministry.

Not knowing what else to do, I opened a drawer and found a Bible I had reluctantly accepted from a campus ministry in the university courtyard a few months earlier. I began to read the Word of Life prayerfully for the first time in years, and light started to break forth. In the following weeks and months, God began to work in my heart. That Christmas, I returned home, and God set me on a new path.

Post tenebras lux—"after darkness, light." In moments of darkness, people are drawn to the light. Against the backdrop of darkness, light shines even brighter. As each Christmas approaches, I am reminded of my journey back to Christ, "the light of the world" (John 9:5). Perhaps you or a loved one is walking in a season of darkness. In moments of difficulty, disease, and even death, it's vital to remember that the God of light is always at work. In him, the darkness cannot overcome, because it does not have the last word (John 1:5). While we may not know what the future holds, we know who holds our futures. And there is no shadow of change in him (James 1:17).

IN HIM, THE DARKNESS
CANNOT OVERCOME,
BECAUSE IT DOES NOT HAVE
THE LAST WORD.

W3 | D4

THE LIGHT OF LIFE

JONI EARECKSON TADA

is founder and CEO of Joni and Friends, an organization that provides Christian outreach in the disability community. Joni is the author of numerous bestselling books, including *Joni and Ken: An Untold Love Story* and *When God Weeps*. Joni and her husband, Ken, reside in Calabasas, California.

When I was a kid, early on Saturday mornings I would gather with neighborhood friends, and—with our parents' permission—we would ride the streetcar up to the Ambassador Theatre in Gwynn Oak Junction, Baltimore. When the movie was about to begin, we had to walk through a thick velvet curtain to enter the theater. Immediately, we'd bump up against the back row. Only after our eyes adjusted to the dark could we find our seats.

After the show was over, again there was no vestibule to ease ourselves out of darkness and into the light of day. The sun was so dazzling outside that we'd stumble, rub our eyes, and try not to bump into things. The brilliance was a jolt to our senses.

I often think about that experience when I read 1 Peter 2:9, "Proclaim the excellencies of him who called you out of darkness into his marvelous light" (ESV). The spiritual contrast Peter is explaining here is akin to exiting a pitch-black theater and being hit with blinding sunlight.

This verse also describes the jolt I felt when God called me out of my own darkness. You see, more than five decades ago, I broke my neck in a diving accident that left me a quadriplegic. Without use of my hands or legs, I plummeted into deep depression, convinced that God had abandoned me. The depression was like a thick darkness, and it lasted a long time.

W3 D4

Then, Christian friends opened the Bible and shone into my soul John 8:12, where Jesus said, "I am the light of the world. Whoever follows me will never walk in darkness, but will have the light of life."

It sounded hopeful, and I wanted to believe, yet Jesus' claim seemed audacious. But a friend explained, "If Jesus loved you enough to die a torturous death to save you, then doesn't that prove he is trustworthy? That his intentions for you are good?"

It was a jolt to my senses—like parting a heavy curtain and stepping out into a light so bright it illuminated everything. I realized God took no pleasure in my paralysis, but it was part of his mysterious yet trustworthy plan for my life. When the eyes of my heart adjusted to God's hope-filled light, I felt as though I had awakened from a long nightmare. And although I would remain paralyzed in a wheelchair, my soul would never be the same. God had "called [me] out of darkness into his marvelous light." It was just like Jesus shouting into a dark grave, "Lazarus, come out!" (John 11:43).

It's why I love Advent. The world was impossibly dark before the birth of Christ. But then the Light of the World arrived, changing everything. Advent reminds us that "the true light that gives light to everyone [has come] into the world" (John 1:9). During this dark-become-light season, part the curtain and hear Christ's call: "Come out!" Then, step into the sunshine of his glorious salvation.

I REALIZED GOD TOOK NO PLEASURE IN MY PARALYSIS, BUT IT WAS PART OF HIS MYSTERIOUS YET TRUSTWORTHY PLAN FOR MY LIFE.

W3|D5

ENDURANCE AND REDEMPTION

NANA DOLCE

(MTS) is the author of *You Are Redeemed* and *The Seed of the Woman*. She is a guest lecturer at the Reformed Theological Seminary in Washington, DC, and a Charles Simeon Trust instructor. Nana lives in Washington, DC, with her husband and four children.

I gave birth to my adopted son last year. He was born at home before dawn on a warm August morning. I carried him for 38 weeks—still, he was conceived years before his days in my womb. I delivered a baby in 2024 whose life began in the year 2003.

Mercedes Luna-Munroe was born in New York to Dominican parents. She met her first husband when she was 25. She remembers the day he walked into her parents' home. The year was 1998. A stranger on an errand, he came to pick up empanadas from her mom and left an impression behind. The stranger became her friend and then her husband in 2000. Sadly, difficulty would devour the young marriage.

Mercedes heard the dreadful word "infertile" at age 26. She was diagnosed with polycystic ovarian syndrome and was given few options beyond in vitro fertilization (IVF). She trod the costly road of conceiving children through IVF and welcomed six embryos in April 2003. Although her journey to children should have ended that year, the story had just begun.

Mercedes became pregnant with two of her six embryos—twin girls named Samantha and Lizbeth. Then the unthinkable happened at 23 weeks of gestation. Her cervix dilated prematurely, and her amniotic sac was accidentally punctured during an examination. An untimely labor ended the lives of her twins. The girls, born on August 11, 2003,

W3 D5

lived only a few hours. The traumatic loss of her babies is a heartbreak Mercedes continues to nurse. Her pregnancy with Samantha and Lizbeth would be her last.

Her doctor transferred two additional embryos to her with no positive pregnancy test. By 2005, Mercedes had two remaining embryos and no marriage. Her memories of this period are saturated with dark shadows. She sank into depression while working to maintain her home and preserve her two frozen embryos. When she could no longer afford to pay the storage fees, Mercedes faced two choices: destroy the tiny lives or donate them. She (and her ex-husband) chose the latter. The embryos were shipped to the National Embryo Donation Center (NEDC) in Knoxville, Tennessee. And here, my family enters the story.

I was battling secondary infertility when I learned of NEDC's embryo adoption program. My husband and I applied in early 2023 with the hope of adopting an embryo who had been waiting for a long time. Mercedes' little ones had been frozen for 20 years when we found them. Both embryos were transferred to me in December 2023. One went to be with the Lord; we named him Zion. The other was born on August 11, 2024, and we named him Kian (which means "enduring"). Kian shares a birthday with the twin sisters Mercedes delivered and lost 21 years before.

Kian's middle name is Immanuel, which means "God with us." The name appears in Isaiah 7:14. Israel was threatened by strong enemies and shook with fear like a forest shaken by winds. But God was with his people and promised to save them. His word came with a sign: A son would be born and

> **GOD'S PEOPLE LIVE IN A WORLD WHERE TRAUMATIC HEARTBREAKS LEAVE US SHAKEN. YET OUR GOD IS WITH US IN EVERY DARKNESS.**

named "God is with us" despite the dark circumstances. This sign, partially fulfilled in Isaiah's time, was ultimately satisfied one starlit night in Bethlehem. A virgin conceived and bore a son—Jesus the Messiah (Matt. 1:21–23).

God's people live in a world where traumatic heartbreaks leave us shaken. Yet our God is with us in every darkness. His presence is our light and the source of our hope. I gave birth to an adopted son named Immanuel because the greater Immanuel is a redeemer.

WHEN THE DARKNESS IS INSIDE

RONNI KURTZ

is an assistant professor of systematic theology at Midwestern Baptist Theological Seminary. He is the author of several books, including *Fruitful Theology: How the Life of the Mind Leads to the Life of the Soul* and *Light Unapproachable: Divine Incomprehensibility and the Task of Theology*.

The opening salvo of the biblical narrative exemplifies a truth that runs through the entirety of the unfolding drama: Light will overcome the darkness.

Open the pages of our sacred book and you are at once introduced to the beautiful theme of illumination. Out of nothing, God calls forth the cosmos with its trillions of burning stars, moons, and celestial lights illuminating what was dark before he spoke. Creation inaugurates an economy of light in which darkness will not have the final word, and this theme remains steady as the story unfolds.

We see light overcoming the darkness when God is present with his people as a pillar of fire illuminating the way in the night (Ex. 13:21-22). In the Psalms, we see that both God and his Word illuminate, as the psalmist declares, "The Lord is my light and my salvation—whom shall I fear?" (27:1) and "Your word is a lamp for my feet, a light on my path" (119:105). In the New Covenant, the theme of light is advanced as John writes about the incarnate Christ: "In him was life, and that life was the light of all mankind. The light shines in the darkness, and the darkness has not overcome it" (John 1:4-5). Even those who follow this incarnate, illuminating Christ are called "the light of the world" (Matt. 5:14-16).

These are but a handful of passages in which God emphasizes the power of light over darkness.

W3 D6

All this illuminating beauty—from the burning stars to the light of God's Word—is glorious news, but the good news of God's light does not stop there. These instances of God's illuminating work are all "out there." There is a distance to them. God's breathing burning stars into existence is wonderful beyond description, but many times illumination is most needed not "out there" but rather "in here."

For many of us, a darkness lingers in the crevasse of our souls, showing itself as a crippling feedback loop of self-degradation. It's a chorus, sung on repeat, from my innermost being that reminds me of my brokenness, my unworthiness, and, most often, my being unlovable. For many of us, the gospel is a true, present, and even gorgeous reality that we have no problem believing on behalf of others. I believe that no one is beyond the reach of the gospel's cleansing power. I believe that God not only loves you but even likes you. I believe that, in Christ, you are not an unwanted stepchild but an adopted and cherished son or daughter with bold access to your Father, who will never turn you away. And often, I can believe these realities for you, but the darkness inside makes it difficult to see how any of them can be true for me. This is not humility; it's a perverse inward humiliation in which I sometimes feel as though darkness may have the final word in my self-talk and self-hatred.

Yet God's illuminating work is not confined to the cosmos—as big as it may be. Though it can be a fight to believe at times, God illuminates not only the sky with burning stars in creation but also those dark corners of our souls.

> **GOD ILLUMINATES NOT ONLY THE SKY WITH BURNING STARS IN CREATION BUT ALSO THOSE DARK CORNERS OF OUR SOULS.**

In the darkness-expelling beauty of the gospel, we hear the promise of 1 John 3:20 that even when "our heart condemns us, God is greater than our heart, and he knows everything" (ESV).

The illuminating work of God can be like fireworks that light up the sky and give light to all who look up. But for each of us with a dreadful inner voice, at times the illuminating gospel is more importantly a surgeon, taking the scalpel of Christ's life, death, and victorious resurrection to the inward darkness, the crevasses of the soul. Places we thought were unredeemable, unlovable, and maybe unfindable, God goes even there in his illuminating work of bringing resurrection where there was death. ✳

W3|D7

NO MATTER HOW DARK

RUSS RAMSEY

(MDiv, Taylor University; ThM, Covenant Theological Seminary) is a pastor at Christ Presbyterian Church in Nashville, Tennessee, and the author of several books, including *Van Gogh Has a Broken Heart*.

I spent my 40th birthday in the hospital. This was not my plan.

A fever led to the doctor's office. The doctor's office led to a blood test. The blood test led to a phone call telling me to go to the emergency room; they were waiting for me.

That first day in the hospital was chaotic. The second day was full of testing and radiology. The third day, my birthday, I finally settled in. I spent most of that day waiting for my test results to come back so the doctors could determine how to treat me. I called my wife and asked her to bring the kids.

After I hung up, a cardiac surgeon—a man whom I had not met before but who would soon hold my heart in his hands—dropped by. He told me they had seen an issue on my echocardiogram and explained that I was in the early stages of heart failure and would need open-heart surgery.

This was the first time those words were spoken to me. "When?" I said.

He said, "In a few weeks, once we get your infection under control."

Around the dinner hour, I found myself flipping through the channels. Alone. Struggling. Lost. *It was a fine birthday*, I told myself. *It's okay. You are going to be okay.*

Then came a knock on my door. An older African American woman poked her head in and said, "I have your dinner."

W3 | D7

As she set the tray down on the table beside me, she looked at the number on my ID bracelet and asked me for my name and date of birth. I recited both like I had a hundred times that week.

She nodded, started to leave, and then stopped. "Wait," she said. "Today is your birthday?"

"It is," I said.

She straightened herself up, turned to face me, and put her right hand over her left—a portrait of dignity and poise. And then, with just the two of us in the room, she began to sing over me:

Happy birthday to you.
Happy birthday to you.
Happy birthday, dear Mr. Ramsey.
Happy birthday to you.

I wept.

It was such a dark day. I felt like my life was in the balance, which it was. And with such a simple gesture, that kind woman was a light. She did not know me. She didn't know whether I was kind or mean, gentle or abrasive, honest or a liar. She just knew that since I was there in her hospital on my birthday, I was probably feeling a little lost. I mattered to her.

Advent reminds us that no matter how dark we might sense the world to be, we are known and seen by the God who so wonderfully made us and knows our deepest need—met for us perfectly in the gift of his Son, the Lord Jesus Christ.

NO MATTER HOW DARK WE MIGHT SENSE THE WORLD TO BE, WE ARE KNOWN AND SEEN BY THE GOD WHO SO WONDERFULLY MADE US AND KNOWS OUR DEEPEST NEED.

WEEK 3

REFLECTION

IF I SAY, "SURELY THE DARKNESS SHALL COVER ME, AND THE LIGHT ABOUT ME BE NIGHT," EVEN THE DARKNESS IS NOT DARK TO YOU; THE NIGHT IS BRIGHT AS THE DAY, FOR DARKNESS IS AS LIGHT WITH YOU.

PSALM 139:11-12, ESV

As Christmas Day draws near, what is something that the Lord has been revealing to you about his faithfulness? Take a moment to praise him for some of the ways you've experienced his shepherding heart and fatherly care in this season.

What is one story in particular that stuck out to you during this week's readings? Recount a story in your life that gives testimony to Christ's power to break through the darkness and reveal his merciful light.

Reflect on some areas in your life that seem dark and unclear to you. It could be struggles at work, parenting decisions, marriage difficulties, or financial hardships, just to name a few. Although Christmas cannot eliminate all the conflicts we experience in this fallen world, it does point us to the one who promises to never leave or forsake us through them. How does this good news offer tangible help and hope to you today?

WEEK 4

For outlandish creatures like us, on our way to a heart, a brain, and courage, Bethlehem is not the end of our journey but only the beginning—not home but the place through which we must pass if ever we are to reach home at last.

FREDERICK BUECHNER

Again Jesus spoke to them, saying, "I am the Light of the World. Whoever follows me will not walk in darkness, but will have the Light of Life."

JOHN 8:12

ESV

W4|D1

NIGHT SKIES AND DARK PATHS

SCOTT JAMES

is an elder at The Church at Brook Hills in Birmingham, Alabama, and the author of children's books and family devotionals, including *The Sower*, *The Expected One*, and, releasing in early 2026, *Deep Breath, Little Whisper*. He is also a pediatric doctor.

When I stepped from my tent into total darkness, the night was a void that felt expansive and oppressive all at once. Toeing my way forward, I sensed a canopy of trees above—an imagined imprint of the forest I knew to be there. Before the sun had given way to a lightless crescent moon, I had taken a mental snapshot of my surroundings, and it was with this vague and unfounded sense of direction that I stepped carefully ahead, slow and patient, hands outstretched.

I had the odd realization that it didn't matter where I looked. Eyes forward gave no benefit in this darkness, so I let my purblind gaze wander. As I did, I caught the briefest flicker of light. Somewhere up and far. Angling my head skyward, I caught another pinprick. Stars, here and there, peeking through sprawling tree boughs. Now more appeared, and with increasing regularity the closer I drew to the edge of the woods.

Finally, I shuffled into an open field, and the sky exploded in celestial glory. I was not prepared for the vast greatness of this, the unsullied beauty of a wilderness nightscape. The heavens declared, and I heard it loud and clear.

The eerie thing was, as I gazed upward at the brilliant spectacle, the immediate darkness in which I stood was just as absolute as it had been in the forest. Up there, the stars in their courses lit the sky in galactic explosions.

W4|D1

Down here, I still couldn't see past the end of my nose. I stood in that strange discordance—immersed in the dark yet basking in heavenly light.

I thought of Abraham, the spiritual father of stargazers everywhere. When he stood in the wilderness and tilted his face skyward, surely his nights were darker and his constellations brighter than any we see today. I imagined God calling Abraham, scattering visible signs of kingdom promise across the blue-black sky. *Look to the heavens. Count the stars, if you can; that's how generously I will bless you.* I imagined Abraham's stunned face.

Abraham held a promise as clear as the night sky, but his immediate path still led through dark terrain. He stepped forward in faith, hands outstretched, trusting God to steady his steps when he couldn't see the way. Awash in starlight, Abraham believed God even as he fumbled through the dark. Each flickering star pierced the night, reminding him of the comforting voice that said, "Do not be afraid, Abram. I am your shield" (Gen. 15:1).

Looking to God, trusting him to keep his promises in his own perfect time, Abraham toed his way forward in the darkness of a fallen world, eyes fixed on the inbreaking of God's light. And "Abraham, having patiently waited, obtained the promise" (Heb. 6:15, ESV). Ultimately, all of Abraham's faithful stargazing was fulfilled in Jesus, the Light of the World—the one in whom "all the promises of God find their Yes" (John 8:12; 2 Cor. 1:20, ESV).

This is how we wait too. We stand in the night, gazing up at stars of unfailing promise. Sometimes the darkness

> **SOMETIMES THE DARKNESS OF OUR PATHS IS INCOMPREHENSIBLE, BUT THE FAITHFULNESS OF OUR GUIDE IS UNWAVERING.**

of our paths is incomprehensible, but the faithfulness of our Guide is unwavering. And as we look to Jesus and await his glorious return, we can always trust him to steady our steps and to lead us "out of darkness into his wonderful light" (1 Pet. 2:9).

W4 | D2

IN THE LOOMING DARKNESS, LIGHT

KAREN SWALLOW PRIOR

(PhD) is a popular writer and speaker. A former English professor, Karen is now a contributing writer for *The Dispatch* and a columnist for Religion News Service. Her writing has appeared in *The New York Times*, *The Atlantic*, *Vox*, *The Washington Post*, *Christianity Today*, and many other places. Her most recent book is *You Have a Calling: Finding Your Vocation in the True, Good, and Beautiful* (Brazos, 2025).

I felt like I had been hit by a bus.

Unfortunately, I have been literally hit by a bus, so I know exactly what that feels like. But this was worse than the physical trauma of bleeding parts and broken bones. This was broken trust and a crushed spirit. This metaphorical bus was the trauma of betrayal.

Betrayal breaks things you didn't know could be broken and ushers in losses of things you didn't even know you had until they are gone. The *Encyclopedia of Psychological Trauma* describes betrayal trauma as occurring "when the people or institutions on which a person depends for survival significantly violate that person's trust or well-being." Such treachery is life-altering. It changes not only your external life but your inner life too, making you doubt your own judgment and very beliefs because you misplaced them in the ones who broke your trust.

Jesus knows what it is to be betrayed.

On his way to the cross, where he would endure the worst physical pain possible, Jesus experienced perhaps the worst emotional pain possible.

Jesus was betrayed by a member of his innermost circle, handed over by a friend to enemies for mere silver. The incident took place in the darkness of the garden where he had gone to seek his Father's will and to let his own will be known to God. The sign given for his betrayal was the symbol of love, friendship, and brotherhood: a kiss.

W4|D2

It's hard to imagine a breach of trust deeper than this.

Yet Jesus knew he would be betrayed—and he kept on ministering anyway. Jesus didn't accuse his betrayer but allowed the villainous disciple to accuse himself. At their last meal together before the cross, Jesus told the Twelve that one of them would do this. When Judas asked Jesus if he meant him, Jesus simply replied, "You have said so" (Matt. 26:25). And when Judas came for Jesus in the garden, Jesus said to him quietly, "Do what you came for, friend" (v. 50).

Jesus did not despair. He was not confused. He did not seek vengeance. He even instructed one who drew a sword in his defense to put the weapon away (vv. 51–52).

Jesus let the darkness be the darkness while he kept on being the light.

In the emergency room where I was taken after being struck by the bus, while the doctors did what they needed to do and a friend held my hand, there was a moment when I was overcome by pain. Yet in the looming darkness that swirled around me, I saw a light. In that light I felt the presence of God. I felt a peace I couldn't understand (Phil. 4:7).

Later, in the darkness of betrayal, it was harder to see that light. But it was there. And to that light—to Jesus—I turned. I drew closer to his presence than I'd ever been before. And somehow, I was—and still am—at peace. Because "the light shines in the darkness, and the darkness has not overcome it" (John 1:5).

JESUS LET THE DARKNESS
BE THE DARKNESS WHILE HE
KEPT ON BEING THE LIGHT.

W4|D3

WHAT THEY SEEM

RONNIE MARTIN

is director of leader care and renewal for Harbor Network and pastor in residence at Redeemer Community Church in Bloomington, Indiana.

There was a bike under the tree.

That's what Dad said, anyway. But I didn't see a thing, and I'm pretty sure I had 20/20 vision at 10 years old.

It was the same old yuletide routine with my old man. He began joking on Christmas Eve about what we were getting—and not getting—for Christmas. Our beloved tree sat there, barely upright in all its 1980s glory, gaudy gold tinsel dangling from homemade ornaments that would make any HGTV designer gasp in horror if she could only see it now. But clearly, no bike was lurking under those sad, dying pine needles. Just a gaggle of randomly wrapped presents my grandma had left the week before, none of which were remotely big enough to house any wheels, chains, or handlebars.

I decided to get bold. I asked Dad to promise me that there was a bike under the tree. This would be my ace in the hole, since grown-ups aren't allowed to lie. To my surprise, he uttered the fateful words "I promise you." My 10-year-old brain was dumbfounded. If I had been any good at math like Dad or shown any signs of being a fledgling engineering prodigy, I probably could've easily figured out the mystery. But I was the happy kid who dressed up like Spider-Man and built secret hideaways in our walk-in-closets. You can see my dilemma.

W4|D3

Twelve hours later, in the wee hours of Christmas morning, I practically galloped to the living room with enough energetic glee to power a thousand Christmas trees. Yet there was still no bike under the tree. "I knew it. All men are liars!" I shouted to my oblivious siblings, not realizing my words were a prophetic signpost leading me to a life of preaching in the fairly distant future.

Except here's the thing: There was a bike under the tree after all. My exhausted, 5:00 a.m. coffee-gulping old man told me to go to the garage, open the door to the crawlspace underneath the house, and look under the blanket. Sure enough, there it was in all its brand-new glory and wonder—sitting directly under the floor where that gaudy, almost needleless tree was somehow still standing.

All I can remember thinking at that moment was *It's settled. My father is a bona fide genius. How did he ever dream up a riddle like this?*

Today, I look back fondly at this cherished boyhood memory of Christmas, and I'm reminded that things aren't always what they seem. Even when my lenses have been clouded by the tears of all the sad things 10-year-olds can't imagine they will someday have to endure, I still have a Father who knows how to give good gifts to his children (Matt. 7:11).

Every year, Christmas enters my life like the final page of a novel, where all the dark years and dashed expectations give way to the one thing we dare to hope will come true—and his name is Jesus Christ.

CHRISTMAS ENTERS MY LIFE
LIKE THE FINAL PAGE
OF A NOVEL, WHERE ALL
THE DARK YEARS AND DASHED
EXPECTATIONS GIVE WAY
TO THE ONE THING WE DARE
TO HOPE WILL COME TRUE.

CHRISTMAS TEARS

W4|D4
CHRISTMAS DAY

JONAH SAGE

serves as one of the pastors of Sojourn Church in New Albany, Indiana. He completed his undergraduate studies in philosophy at Miami University (Oxford, Ohio) and received his master of divinity from The Southern Baptist Theological Seminary in 2013.

Nothing represents the mosaic of the human experience quite like the tears of a newborn. Disorientation and discomfort mingle with joy and victory on that little one's cheeks. Soon accompanied by the tears of mother and father, these simple drops of liquid carry all we are and all we hope to be. The infant's cry marks a victory of sorts. New life is here. Hope is here. The little one's future is pregnant with promise. Yet there remains the mother's long road to recovery, the stubbed toes and scraped knees as the toddler learns to walk, the development of language, the gathering of experience, and the inevitable disappointments and losses of later years. The way new life arrived on Christmas morning shows us something of what God feels and intends for us. It shapes the expectations hidden within our imaginations and whispers to us the secret of who we really are.

W4|D4

An infant's tears are a searching for the mother. When God drew near, his first desire was the comforting arms of another. Jesus' tears remind us he came to the world to hold and be held by it. *O Jerusalem*, he later laments, *how I longed to gather you beneath my wings as a hen gathers her chicks* (Matt. 23:37). The infant crying to be held by his mother grew into a man crying to hold us too.

An infant's tears are an announcement that something is wrong. Without vocabulary, all the child can do is cry. The Lord is birthed in solidarity with a world that cannot adequately express the depths of what ails us. There are, as it were, groans deeper than words. But somehow the tears of a baby capture the depth of it well enough. God did not stay in a far-off country but came near to suffer as we do. Jesus knows what it's like to be us.

Jesus' Christmas tears are a reminder that God's promises are always fulfilled. These are not wasted, vain tears. They are the tears of one who has come to carry us to a place where our tears will be wiped away. They are the tears of one who will make a way for us to come home. Christmas reminds us that God took matters into and onto his own hands. The newborn tears of Jesus move us forward to his lonely tears in Gethsemane, his agonized tears on the cross, and perhaps even Mary's despairing tears at the tomb. Jesus' life began and ended with tears so that, through resurrection, our days of tears would be numbered.

This is why we sing "Joy to the world, the Lord is come." He came as a mother to hold a world whose tears are beyond expression. In that warm embrace, he carries us, comforts

> **JESUS' LIFE BEGAN AND ENDED WITH TEARS SO THAT, THROUGH RESURRECTION, OUR DAYS OF TEARS WOULD BE NUMBERED.**

us, strengthens us, and restores us. "Why are you crying?" he gently asks Mary (and us). Just as he did Mary, he will call each of us by name (John 20:15-16). In a flash, in the twinkling of an eye, our tears of labor pain will be replaced by tears of joy. New life is here. Hope is here—our future is now pregnant with promise. Here on this day is all we are and all we will one day become. "Joy to the world, the Lord is come."

WEEK 4

REFLECTION

AGAIN JESUS SPOKE TO THEM, SAYING, "I AM THE LIGHT OF THE WORLD. WHOEVER FOLLOWS ME WILL NOT WALK IN DARKNESS, BUT WILL HAVE THE LIGHT OF LIFE."

JOHN 8:12, ESV

As Christmastime reaches its conclusion this year, take a few minutes to reflect on how you are coming out of it. What are some lingering struggles you are wrestling with as you step into the new year? What is one hope you can bring before the Lord as the new year approaches?

What is one story in particular that stuck out to you during this week's readings? Following Jesus means we will inevitably be confronted with inexplicable trials at times. What do these stories reveal about the light of Jesus during times of darkness and distress?

As you anticipate the new year, what are some truths God has reminded you of during this Advent season that will bring some welcomed assurance of his presence? Take a moment to rejoice in Christ, confess your sins, thank him for his forgiveness, and ask for renewed strength to follow him.

NOTES

NOTES